Florence Nightingale

John Malam

Heinemann Library
Chicago, Illinois

© 2001 Reed Educational & Professional Publishing
Published by Heinemann Library,
an imprint of Reed Educational & Professional Publishing,
Chicago, IL
Customer Service 888-454-2279

Visit our website at www.heinemannlibrary.com

Designed by Tessa Barwick
Illustrated by Michael Posen
Originated by Ambassador Litho
Printed in Hong Kong

05 04 03 02 01
10 9 8 7 6 5 4 3 2 1

Library of Congress Cataloging-in-Publication Data

Malam, John, 1957-
    Florence Nightingale / John Malam
        p. cm. -- (Groundbreakers)
    Includes bibliographical references and index.
    ISBN 1-58810-051-0
    1. Nightingale, Florence, 1820-1910--Juvenile literature. 2.
    Nurses--England--Biography--Juvenile literature. [1. Nightingale, Florence, 1820-1910.
    2. Nurses. 3. Women--Biography.] I. Title. II. Series.

RT37.N5 M35 2001
610.73'092--dc21
[B]
                                                        00-061387

Acknowledgments
The author and publishers are grateful to the following for permission to reproduce copyright material: Art Archive, p. 28; Bridgeman Art Library/Royal Holloway and Bedford New College, Surrey, UK, p. 12; The Florence Nightingale Museum, pp. 4, 5, 6, 9, 10, 14, 22, 24, 25, 30, 31, 32, 33, 34, 35, 36, 37, 38, 39, 40, 41; Hulton Getty, pp. 7, 8, 19, 26, 27; John and Hilary Malam, pp. 15, 29; Mary Evans Picture Library, pp. 17, 20, 23; MPM Images, p. 16; National Portrait Gallery, p. 11; P&O Art Collection, p. 21; Science Photo Library, p. 42; Science Photo Library/James King-Holmes, p. 43; Simon Fraser/Wellcome Library, London, p. 13.
Cover photograph reproduced with the permission of Mary Evans Picture Library.

Every effort has been made to contact copyright holders of any material reproduced in this book. Any omissions will be rectified in subsequent printings if notice is given to the publisher.

Some words are shown in bold, **like this.** You can find out what they mean by looking in the glossary.

Contents

Who Was Florence Nightingale?

The world is the way it is because of what people have done in the past. Our lives have been changed by inventions and discoveries. However, these are not the only things that have shaped our world. One of the greatest ways society develops is by changing the way we think about something, and the people who succeed in bringing about change are called **reformers.**

A great reformer

One such reformer was Florence Nightingale, a British woman who lived in the 1800s. From an early age, Florence knew that she wanted to work among the poor and the sick. Her parents were horrified when she told them she wanted to become a nurse. At the time, nursing was not a respectable occupation for women who, like Florence, came from wealthy families. However, she was determined to follow her calling, not the wishes of her parents. Eventually, she did become a nurse.

This painting from 1855 shows Florence Nightingale visiting soldiers in a hospital during the Crimean War.

A turning point

Wars often change society in useful ways as well as harmful ones. For example, the American Civil War led to the abolition of slavery in the United States. The Crimean war allowed Florence Nightingale to make hospitals healthier and safer places. In the mid–1850s, Britain was at war in the Crimea, a region in southern Russia. Florence went there with a group of nurses. She cared for sick and wounded soldiers, and improved the conditions of the military hospitals there.

In Britain, after the war, Florence set up the Nightingale Training School. It taught women about nursing and trained them to be nurses. She wrote a groundbreaking book that described how she thought nursing should be done. Little by little, Florence laid the foundations for nursing as we know it today.

This photograph of Florence Nightingale was taken in 1856, when she was 36 years old.

THE LADY WITH A LAMP

In 1857, the American poet Henry Longfellow (1807–82) wrote a poem about Florence Nightingale. Here is one of its verses:

Lo! in that house of misery
A lady with a lamp I see
Pass through the glimmering gloom,
And flit from room to room.

Longfellow's poem described Florence as "a lady with a lamp." Ever since, this is how she has been remembered, walking the dark corridors and gloomy wards of her battlefield hospital, with the flickering light of a lamp showing the way ahead.

Florence Nightingale was a remarkable woman. She worked hard to overcome the **prejudices** people had about nursing, and about the role of women in British society. Her gift to the present-day world is something we cannot now live without—nursing is accepted as an essential part of modern society.

Florence Is Born

This photograph shows William and Frances Nightingale, Florence's parents, in their old age.

In the early nineteenth century, it was fashionable for wealthy British people to travel to the cities of Europe. The tourists of the early 1800s did not visit these places for just a few weeks like vacationers today, but might stay overseas for months, and even years at a time.

Florence's parents in Italy

Florence Nightingale's life story begins on just such a foreign trip. In 1818, her parents, William and Frances "Fanny" Nightingale, left Britain to visit Italy. They were wealthy, and could stay away from Britain for a long time if they wanted to, since neither of them had to work for a living. In Italy, the Nightingales visited ancient ruins and churches adorned with wonderful paintings. For the newly-married couple, this was a chance to see famous works of art and architecture firsthand.

FLORENCE'S PARENTS

Fl[...] ore (1794–1874).
W[...] ne from his uncle,
Pe[...] erbyshire,
a[...] and the land
be[...] f his generous
re[...] hore to
N[...] ce Nightingale
w[...]

Fl[...] 880), known to
ev[...] n and was the
da[...] upbringing, and
w[...]

[Handwritten note:] Florence's parents were William & Frances (Fanny) Nightingale.

An unusual name

In 1819, William and Frances were staying in Naples, a city in southern Italy. It was here that their first child was born. They named the baby girl Parthenope, the ancient Greek name for Naples, her birthplace. It was an unusual name, and it was often shortened to Parthe or Pop.

The following year, the family traveled to the north of Italy, where they rented a house on the outskirts of the city of Florence. It was here that their second daughter was born, on May 12, 1820. Like Parthenope, this girl was also named after the city of her birth, and this is how Florence Nightingale got her first name. It, too, was an unusual name at the time, and it was not long before people began to call her Flo for short.

This is how Florence, the Italian city where Florence Nightingale was born, looked in the early 1800s.

At Home in England

In 1821, when Florence was a year old, her family left Italy. They had lived there for almost three years. Florence's father would have been happy to stay in Italy for longer, but her mother felt it was time they returned home to England.

Florence (left), about age sixteen, stitches embroidery with her sister, Parthenope.

Two homes

Florence's father had inherited an old house from his uncle, Peter Nightingale. The house at Lea, in Derbyshire, England, was in poor condition, and not suitable for the Nightingale family, their maids, footmen, coachmen, and cook. Instead, Florence's father had a new house built nearby, and named it Lea Hurst. No sooner had the family moved in than Florence's mother realized it was a mistake. Lea Hurst would not make a good family home after all. It was a long way from London, and she was worried that no one would visit. Even though the house had fifteen bedrooms, she thought it was too small. Worse still, it was cold, and both Florence and Parthenope became ill with **bronchitis.** In 1825, when Florence was five years old, her father bought Embley Park, a house near Romsey in Hampshire. This house was closer to London, and was therefore much better for the family.

In Nightingale's words:

"I craved for some regular occupation, for something worth doing instead of frittering [wasting] time away on useless trifles [unimportant things]."

(From a private note. Florence jotted down many of her thoughts throughout her life. These notes provide us with a real insight into her private life.)

This picture of Embley Park, the family home in Hampshire, was drawn by Parthenope, who was a talented artist.

Florence's childhood

In summer, Florence lived with her family at Lea Hurst. Embley Park was the family home in winter. There were visits to London, cousins came to stay, and she dressed well and ate good food. Florence should have been overjoyed at this fortunate lifestyle, but in later life, she said that she had disliked it. Like many girls from respectable families at the time, Florence and her sister Parthe were educated at home. A **governess** taught them music and drawing, and once Florence was twelve, their father taught them Greek, Latin, German, French, Italian, grammar, history, mathematics, and **philosophy.** Parthe preferred being in the garden with her mother to doing schoolwork with her father. But Florence was a good pupil. She particularly enjoyed mathematics. When she became a teenager, people noticed that she did not like to talk with others. Instead, she preferred to be on her own, free to drift off into a secret dreamworld. She also developed a passion for neatness and accuracy. A visitor once said that Florence was "extraordinary," suggesting that even at this age, there was something different, something special about her.

EDUCATION AT THE TIME

ys

e
d.

six

Becoming an Adult

Parthenope drew Florence as a young woman, with her pet owl, Athena.

Florence was becoming an adult. She was well-educated and attractive, and her parents were sure she would make a fine wife someday. They started to plan her future and prepared for her **"coming out"**—a custom in those times. This involved holding house parties, dinners, and balls in their home at Embley Park. On these occasions, Florence would be introduced to the guests. It was a way of showing that she was no longer a child. But Florence still held on to things that adults thought of as childish. She had not grown out of her habit of daydreaming—if anything, her dreamworld had become more important to her. It felt real, not like something she created in her mind.

"COMING OUT"

For many years, it was the custom in Britain for girls from wealthy families to "come out." Each year, there was a season of social events, such as dances and parties. Girls, most about the age of eighteen, attended these events, where they were presented to the host. It was an important occasion in the girls' lives—they had "come out" of childhood and were now adults.

Choosing a purpose

On February 7, 1837, when Florence was at home at Embley Park, she had an experience that was to change the course of her life. She had what can only be described as a mystical experience. Perhaps she had drifted into her private world of dreams. She believed she heard voices in her head calling to her. Florence thought that this was a sign from God, and that He had chosen her for a purpose.

Whatever that purpose was, it was not made clear to Florence at that time. She was sixteen, a young woman with the rest of her life ahead of her.

Admirers

Florence had several admirers. Henry Nicholson, one of her cousins, fell in love with her. But although they had many things in common, such as a love of mathematics, Florence had no intention of marrying him. In 1842, she met Richard Monckton Milnes. Eleven years older than Florence, he was rich, intelligent, and fun to be with. They were well matched and they loved each other, but marriage was out of the question for Florence. She believed that for her to do God's work—whatever that was going to be—she must remain unmarried.

Richard Monckton Milnes (1809–85) was one of Florence's admirers. They remained friends for life.

An Interest in Social Issues

Florence's parents hoped she would find a suitable husband, have children, entertain guests, and do all the things that were expected of a woman in polite society. Florence went to dances and the theater, and she loved music. But there was more to life for Florence than music and dancing. She had become interested in social issues, such as poverty and health care. Sometimes, when Florence stayed at Lea Hurst, she went to the homes of sick people in the nearby village. She had found an interest in nursing the sick and needy.

A hospital in Germany

Florence longed to meet people with whom she could have intelligent conversations. In 1842, she was introduced to Christian Bunsen, the Prussian **ambassador** in London. He was a **scholar,** and before long, Florence was a frequent visitor to his house. She borrowed his books and discussed **archaeology** and religion with him.

People line up outside a hospital in the early 1800s. Seriously ill patients were often turned away, for fear that they would bring infections into the hospital.

It was at one of these meetings that he told her about the Institution of **Deaconesses** at the town of Kaiserswerth, near Düsseldorf in Prussia, which is now part of Germany. The Institution was, in part, a hospital with trained nurses. Florence was fascinated—the idea that nursing was a subject that could be taught was entirely new to her.

This cartoon of the 1840s shows a nurse as an uncaring, untidy woman.

In her early twenties, Florence began to sense what God's purpose for her was—she was now certain that God wanted her to be a nurse. In 1844, an American **philanthropist,** Dr. Samuel Gridley Howe, visited the Nightingale family. Florence asked him if he thought it would be "a dreadful thing" if she were to devote her life to nursing. He replied that it would be "a very good thing." The idea of working in nursing began to take shape in her mind.

A family quarrel

Florence knew that her parents would not allow her to go to Kaiserswerth, so she did not ask them. Instead, in 1845, she asked if she could visit the nearby hospital in Salisbury. It would only be for three months, she said, just long enough for her to learn the day-to-day work of nursing. Florence's parents were horrified. At that time, a hospital was no place for a respectable woman. Florence's mother was ashamed of her, and her father thought her education had been wasted. Parthenope was extremely upset. Not surprisingly, Florence was told she could not go.

> **In Nightingale's words:**
>
> *"You don't think that I'm going to stay dangling about my mother's drawing room all my life. I shall go out to work, to be sure."*
>
> (From a private note)

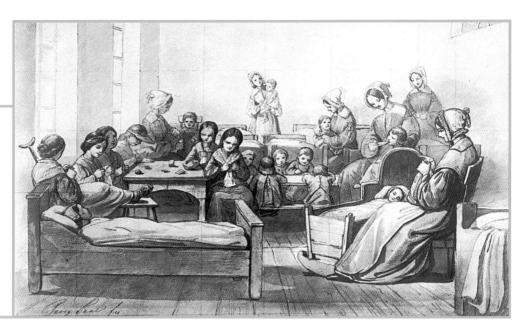

These nurses are caring for children in the children's ward at Kaiserswerth Hospital, Prussia.

In the 1840s, towns in Britain had poor **sanitation.** Diseases, such as **cholera,** spread quickly. The government looked at the situation and issued regular reports. Florence read them in secret. Each day, starting before dawn, she made detailed notes of what she learned, and produced tables of **statistics** that showed facts and figures at a glance. Florence also wrote to experts in France and Prussia. As her knowledge of sanitation increased, she became an expert on the subject. But Florence kept these studies secret from her family.

Helpful friends

As the round of house parties and socializing continued, Florence was torn between her family life and the life she wanted for herself. In 1847, she became ill, with headaches, **bronchitis,** and coughs. She was afraid she was losing her mind. Family friends, Charles and Selina Bracebridge, suggested she travel with them to Italy. Florence's family thought it would do her good. It did, and for a while, she was happy. While in Italy, she met a British politician, Sidney Herbert, and his wife, Elizabeth. They became good friends.

Florence returned home, but it was not long before she was sick once again. She felt low in spirit for months, until the Bracebridges again came to her rescue.

Florence went on another foreign tour with them. For Florence, the highlight was traveling through Prussia. The Bracebridges knew that Florence was interested in nursing, and when she said she wanted to visit the hospital at Kaiserswerth, they did not try to stop her. Florence arrived there on July 31, 1850, and stayed there for two weeks.

The hospital at Kaiserswerth was founded in 1833 by Pastor Theodor Fliedner. He started it as an orphanage, and it grew to include a school and a hospital. In 1851, when Florence Nightingale trained there, the hospital had beds for 100 patients who were cared for by 27 nurses. Women from all over Prussia went to Kaiserswerth to be trained as nurses. They worked hard, from 5 A.M. until late at night, stopping only to eat and pray.

In Nightingale's words:

"*[Kaiserswerth] is my home, there are my brothers and sisters all at work. There my heart is and there, I trust, will one day be my body.*"

(From a private note in which Florence confided her hopes to visit the hospital at Kaiserswerth)

It was here at the Institution of **Deaconesses** at Kaiserswerth, Prussia, that Florence trained to be a nurse.

Being punished

When Florence's parents discovered that she had been to Kaiserswerth, they were furious. As a punishment, Florence had to work as her sister's servant for six months. Women from wealthy families at the time did not go to work, and remained dependent on their parents until they married. Florence was 30 years old, yet her parents still treated her like a naughty child. In her heart, she knew she could not change the way they felt. She decided to take matters into her own hands. In 1851, after her "slavery" to Parthenope was over, Florence returned to Kaiserswerth. She went alone and stayed for three months. Whether her parents liked it or not, Florence was going to train to be a nurse.

1 Harley Street, London

Harley Street, London, was where Florence worked as a nurse in a small hospital. This is how it looks today.

The reaction from Florence's parents when she returned home from Kaiserswerth was what she expected. "They would hardly speak to me," she wrote. Parthenope, who resented her younger sister's growing independence, had a **nervous breakdown.** It was Florence who nursed her back to health.

Independence

In April 1853, Florence's friend, Elizabeth Herbert, wrote to her and told her that a **superintendent** was needed to run the Institution for the Care of Sick Gentlewomen in Distressed Circumstances. This was a small, private hospital in London. Florence was interviewed and was offered the job. She would have complete control of the hospital, and would be allowed to live in the hospital, although she would not be paid.

The news that Florence had accepted the job caused yet another family argument. Her mother fainted, and Parthe became so upset that she collapsed and was put to bed. Florence's father retreated to his private club. Eventually, however, he decided to help her. He gave her an allowance that was enough for her to live on. At 33, Florence was finally accepted by her family as an adult, and on August 12, 1853, she began her nursing work in earnest.

From house to hospital

The hospital that Florence was to run was moving to a new site, at 1 Harley Street, London. This building had been a private house, and Florence had just ten days to turn it into a hospital. She introduced new ideas, such as putting bells by the patients' beds. When a bell was rung, a valve popped open to show the nurse which patient had called for help. Florence's main problem was a shortage of good nurses—the women who worked at the hospital had not been properly trained.

Florence worked in Harley Street for fourteen months. It was an important time in her life. Not only did she put her nursing skills to use, but she also showed that she was good at organizing.

Inside a Harley Street doctor's consulting rooms in the 1800s, two doctors and a matron are discussing treatment for a patient.

War in the Crimea

In March 1854, Britain and France joined Turkey in declaring war on Russia. They wanted to stop Russia from gaining control of Bulgaria and the Balkans, and from occupying Constantinople, now called Istanbul, in Turkey. A large **peninsula** in southern Russia, almost completely surrounded by inland seas, became the war's main battlefield. The peninsula was called the Crimea, so the war fought there from 1854 to 1856 was the Crimean War.

No one to care for the troops

The British soldiers who fought in the war were transported to the Crimea by troop ships. It was a remote place, about 1,500 miles (2,400 kilometers) away from Britain. The first troops landed at Varna, a town in Bulgaria. In the dirty conditions of the troops' camp, an **epidemic** of the killer disease **cholera** broke out. From there, the army of 27,000 men was hastily transported across the Black Sea to the Crimea, leaving much-needed medical supplies and provisions behind. The army arrived in the Crimea on September 14, 1854, and six days later fought a Russian army in the Battle of the Alma. It was a British victory, but what should have been cause for national celebration soon became a terrible scandal, as people at home learned that the sick and injured soldiers had not been properly cared for.

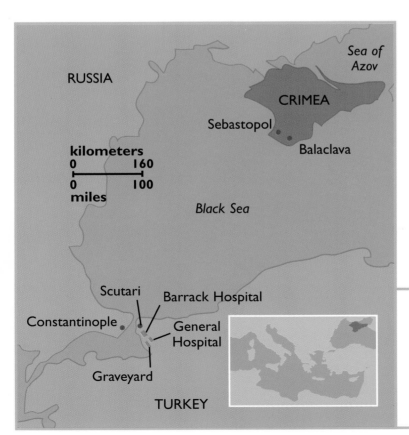

The Crimean peninsula is surrounded by the Black Sea and the Sea of Azov. Today, it is part of the Ukraine.

Reporting the war

The Crimean War was the first war that photographers and newspaper reporters witnessed in detail. It was also the first war in which the **telegraph** was used by reporters to send their **dispatches,** or reports, back to their offices. For the first time, the true horror of war touched people far away from the action as they read about it in their newspapers. Writing in the *Times* on October 12, 1854, war reporter William Russell said: "It is with feelings of surprise and anger that the public will learn that no sufficient preparations have been made for the care of the wounded. Not only are there not sufficient surgeons... no nurses... there is not even linen to make bandages."

William Russell was a journalist whose reports in the Times *newspaper brought home the horror of war and the conditions of the troops in the Crimea.*

Russell's dispatches were highly critical of the British army, and they caused shock and outrage. Florence Nightingale read Russell's reports, and understood the need for better medical care in the army. But she could never have predicted how deeply involved she would become.

WILLIAM RUSSELL—WAR REPORTER

Born in Ireland, William Russell (1821–1907) became the world's first official war correspondent when he reported on the Crimean War. He wrote for the *Times,* one of Britain's most respected daily newspapers. After that war, Russell reported on other conflicts around the world, including the American Civil War (1861–65). In 1895, he was knighted by Queen Victoria. From then on, he was known as Sir William Russell.

Florence Goes to Turkey

The news reports of the Crimean War shocked Britain into action. The *Times* newspaper set up a fund to raise money to buy medical supplies. People wrote angry letters to the newspapers. One letter to the *Times* demanded to know why no nurses had been sent to care for the British soldiers.

A government request

The letter was read by Sidney Herbert, Florence's old friend, who was now the government's **secretary-at-war.** Since the news about the dreadful conditions of the troops in the Crimea had become public knowledge, Herbert was under pressure to do something about the situation. On October 15, 1854, he wrote to Florence to ask her, on behalf of the British government, to take charge of the army's hospitals that had been set up in Turkey. He wrote, "There is but one person in England that I know of who would be capable of organizing and **superintending** such a scheme." It was a challenge that Florence readily accepted. She gave up her job at the Harley Street hospital, and began planning for her trip.

SIDNEY HERBERT—POLITICIAN

Born into an **aristocratic** family, Sidney Herbert (1810–61), was elected the member of Parliament for South Wiltshire when he was only 22 years old. He was a highly capable politician, and was given special responsibility for the British armed forces. As secretary-at-war, he was the government official in overall charge of the army finances during the Crimean War. He made important changes that resulted in improved sanitary conditions and education for the forces. In 1861, he became Lord Herbert of Lea.

The journey to Turkey

It was decided that 40 nurses should go with Florence, but only fourteen could be found who had any experience working in hospitals. In the end, Florence gathered together 38 women—a mixture of nurses and nuns. The nurses were paid more than hospital nurses in London were paid at the time. Uniforms were quickly made for them, and on October 21, less than a week after Florence had been put in charge, the party left London. They travelled to the port of Marseilles, in the south of France, where they boarded a ship called the *Vectis*. On November 4, they reached Scutari, a village in Turkey near the Black Sea. It was here that the British army had set up several hospitals for soldiers wounded in the Crimea, about 350 miles (560 kilometers) to the north. This was where Florence was going to work.

The Vectis carried Florence and her nurses to Scutari. The ship was infested with cockroaches, and Florence was seasick.

In Nightingale's words:

"I do not say that I believe the Times *accounts, but I do believe that we may be of use to the wounded wretches."*

(From a letter to her friend, Elizabeth Herbert, October 14, 1854)

A Hospital at Scutari

The British called their main hospital at Scutari the Barrack Hospital. It had originally been built as a **barracks** for soldiers of the Turkish army, but since the beginning of the Crimean War, it had been converted into a hospital for British soldiers. It was run by officials and doctors of the British army. The building was very large—a great square with a tower at each corner. Inside was a maze of rooms laid out along several miles of hallways.

BATTLE OF BALACLAVA

Balaclava, a port in the Crimea, was captured by the British early in the Crimean War. On October 25, 1854, Russian forces fought the British army at Balaclava, and many soldiers were injured or killed on both sides. The battle became infamous because a misunderstanding of orders sent a British **cavalry regiment** charging straight into the Russian guns. Of the 673 soldiers who took part in the "Charge of the Light Brigade," as it came to be known, 272 died in the battle. Many more were injured and transported by ship to the Barrack Hospital at Scutari.

In spite of feeling sick from the sea voyage, Florence was eager to begin her work at the Barrack Hospital as soon as she could. She went to the hospital on November 5, 1854, the day after she had arrived in Turkey. Conditions inside the hospital were far worse than she could ever have imagined. There was no furniture or anything to cook with, trash was scattered around, the toilets were blocked, and there were rats everywhere. It was in these dreadful conditions that Florence and her nurses were expected to live and work.

This was the Barrack Hospital at Scutari, Turkey. Florence sought to improve conditions for soldiers who were patients here.

Women made **lint** for dressings at British factories like this one. From here, it was shipped out to the Crimea.

Conflict with doctors

In her first few days at Scutari, the work that Florence did was not the nursing she had expected. She was not accepted by the male doctors in the hospital. They were in overall charge, and they resented women being sent to work with them. At first, they refused to allow Florence and her nurses to have anything to do with the patients. The doctors regarded the patients as their responsibility.

In spite of the difficult atmosphere, Florence stayed calm. She set her nurses to cleaning linen, making pillows, and preparing slings for broken limbs. Floors were scrubbed, and the kitchens were cleaned. Then ships began arriving with soldiers who had been wounded at the Battle of Balaclava. The hospital was already filled with about 1,700 patients, and room had to be made for the 500 new arrivals. The doctors still believed they could cope on their own.

In Nightingale's words:

"… these colossal calamities, as the hospitals of Scutari will come to be called in history."

(From a letter to her mother, in which she described the appalling conditions in the hospitals at Scutari, February 1, 1855)

The Lady with a Lamp

This 1855 painting shows Florence Nightingale in the Barrack Hospital at Scutari.

As the sick and injured from Balaclava were admitted to the Barrack Hospital, it became clear that the doctors could not cope without extra help. Reluctantly, they were forced to admit they needed Florence Nightingale and her nurses. It was time for Florence to begin her real work.

In Nightingale's words:

"As I went my night-rounds among the newly-wounded that first night, there was not one murmur, not one groan."

(From a letter to her parents, November 14, 1854)

Florence takes charge

To Florence, who was used to neatness and order, the Barrack Hospital was a place of chaos. No one seemed in charge, there were not enough supplies, and the hospital was filthy. The British army officials who should have been running the hospital were overworked and had almost run out of money.

The doctors and hospital officials soon realized that Florence had access to money that had been raised by the *Times* newspaper. It was enough to buy the supplies they needed. Each day, Florence drew up a list of what was needed, and the supplies were bought in the markets at nearby Constantinople.

The goods went into the hospital's supply rooms, and were issued by Florence when she was asked for them. Before long, if anything was needed, the best thing to do was to "go to Miss Nightingale." Florence's skill at organizing things meant that by December 1854, she was in charge of the hospital's supplies. With enough food, medicine, and bedding, conditions for the patients gradually improved.

The soldiers' gratitude

Each night, Florence walked the gloomy hospital corridors, carrying a lamp to light her way. As the men became used to seeing her, they nicknamed her "the lady with a lamp." It was a term of affection that the American poet Henry Longfellow used in his poem about Florence Nightingale. It was said that the men became so devoted to Florence that they even stopped swearing—something they used to do often—and that they kissed her shadow as it passed over them.

Florence carried a Turkish lantern like this. Inside was a single candle whose light shone through the linen sides.

MARY SEACOLE—THE OTHER LADY WITH A LAMP

Mary Seacole (1805–81) was another nurse who cared for the wounded of the Crimean War. Born in Jamaica, she trained as a **doctress,** like her mother. At her own expense, Mary traveled from Jamaica to the Crimea. On the way, she stopped at Scutari, where she met Florence Nightingale. Mary described her as "a slight figure... with a pale, gentle, and firm face." From Scutari, Mary went to the Crimea, where she set up the British Hotel at Balaclava. Sick and **convalescing** soldiers came there to be cared for. Mary fed them, gave them medicine, and dressed their wounds. The soldiers called her Mother Seacole. The *Times* newspaper said, "A more skillful hand about a wound or a broken limb could not be found."

Florence Makes Changes

Meals for patients were prepared in bulk in kitchens like this one at Scutari.

Florence Nightingale's organizational skills were essential to the running of the Barrack Hospital. She drew up a strict timetable for her nurses. The day began at 8 A.M. with prayers, followed by breakfast. At 9 A.M., a bell rang, and they went to the wards, the kitchen, or the supply room or market. Work stopped at 2 P.M. for lunch. It began again at 4:30 P.M., and continued until 7 P.M., when there was a break for the evening meal, followed by prayers. Florence said that no nurse should be on the wards after 8 P.M. Night duties were carried out by male **orderlies.** The only nurse at night was Florence, who patrolled the hospital's corridors. It was not unusual for her to have just four hours' sleep before beginning another long day on duty.

Improved sanitation

Clean sheets and kind words from Florence were not enough to save soldiers from dying. The hospital was still filthy, and disease spread quickly. The biggest killer was **cholera.** Florence was concerned about the hospital's lack of clean water, its blocked toilets, and its poor drainage.

Florence suspected that germs bred and infections spread under these filthy conditions. She pleaded with the authorities, and finally, a **Sanitary Commission** was set up to look into the importance of hospital cleanliness. Repairs were made to the drains, and the water supply was improved. The death rate fell almost immediately. Before Florence's changes came into force, about 40 percent of patients died. Afterward, the number of deaths fell to about 2 percent.

Florence falls ill

In May 1855, conditions at the Barrack Hospital had improved, and Florence visited the Crimea. She inspected field hospitals and went to meet soldiers on the front lines. Then she fell ill with **"Crimean fever,"** and the doctors feared she might die. Florence recovered, but instead of returning to Britain, she went back to Scutari to continue her work there. It was only when the war ended, in March 1856, that Florence felt free to leave. She returned to Britain, arriving home that August.

This is Alexis Soyer, the hospital chef.

ALEXIS SOYER—CHEF

The food ration each day for a British soldier was 1 pound (about half a kilogram) of meat and bread, with a little coffee, sugar, salt, and water. There were few vegetables. At Scutari, a French chef named Alexis Soyer (1809–58) was invited by Florence to make nourishing meals for the patients. In particular, they were fed beef and mutton soups. Soyer trained soldiers to work as cooks, and taught them to prepare meals in bulk, so they could cook for thousands of patients at a time.

A National Heroine

In Nightingale's words:

"The publicity and talk there have been about this work [at Scutari] have injured it more than anything else, and in no way... will I contribute by making a show of myself."

(From a private note, outlining her reasons for shunning the public, August 1856)

Florence Nightingale's work in the Crimea became well known in Britain. Soldiers spoke of her with great affection, and the government praised her. Sidney Herbert, the official who had asked her to take charge of the army's hospitals in Turkey, called her a "diamond." Florence had become a national heroine, but she did not want publicity.

A royal request

When Florence returned to Britain, she moved back in with her parents and sister. Florence received thousands of letters. There were letters from men asking her to marry them, letters begging for money, and some with strange requests—one man asked her to give him a donkey! Parthenope often replied to these letters on Florence's behalf. Florence was asked to speak at meetings and accept awards, but she refused them all. However, there was one invitation she could not turn down—a request to meet Queen Victoria. In September 1856, Florence met her at Balmoral, the queen's Scottish home.

This brooch is similar to the one Prince Albert designed for Queen Victoria to give to Florence.

Many people would have been stuck for words, but Florence knew exactly what to say. She spoke softly and clearly about the problems in the army's hospital system, especially the poor standards of **hygiene** and diet. The queen listened, and agreed with Florence. With the queen on her side, there would be little to prevent Florence from getting exactly what she believed was needed. Florence wanted a **royal commission** to be set up to investigate the health of the British army. She was determined to **reform** the way the army cared for sick and wounded men.

Another illness

In 1857, Florence became ill. She felt tired and weak, and she lost weight. She was told she was working too hard and should rest. At the time, no one could understand what her illness was. Florence referred to it as her "thorn in the flesh." Today, some doctors believe she was suffering from the aftereffects of seeing terrible pain and suffering during the Crimean War. Doctors today call this condition **post-traumatic stress disorder.**

This pottery model shows Florence and a wounded soldier. Figures like this were bought by ordinary people as souvenirs of their heroine.

POST-TRAUMATIC STRESS DISORDER

Post-traumatic stress disorder (PTSD) affects people after they have experienced a life-threatening event. This can be war, a natural disaster, a serious accident, or a personal assault. PTSD sufferers may relive their experience through nightmares and flashbacks, have difficulty sleeping, and feel detached from everyday life. They may have headaches, stomach complaints, and feelings of dizziness. Research has shown that women are more likely than men to suffer from PTSD.

The Health of the Army

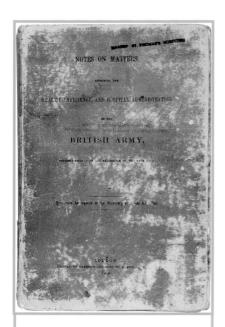

Florence's 1,000-page report was called Notes on Matters affecting the Health, Efficiency and Hospital Administration of the British Army.

A **royal commission** was set up to examine the health of the British army. Florence chose men who were experts in subjects such as **statistics** and **sanitation** to work for the commission; women were not allowed to be commissioners. Sidney Herbert, Florence's good friend, was the chairman.

Prevention is better than cure

In 1858, Florence completed the report of her investigation's results. It contained almost 1,000 pages, crammed with facts and statistics. The report looked at the way the British army had organized its hospitals during wars and also in peacetime. Page after page told the same sad story—that most of the army's deaths, in war and in peace, were caused by poor **hygiene.** Florence noted that army doctors were trained to work as surgeons. They were not trained to prevent disease. Florence decided that prevention is better than cure. She said that soldiers should be given good food, clothing, and shelter, and that they should live in clean, hygienic conditions. If the army treated its men well, they were less likely to become sick. Florence had gathered information about the main diseases that affected the army, particularly infectious ones that spread in dirty conditions, such as **cholera, typhoid,** and **dysentery.** She knew that improved hygiene and better organization of the army's camps, **barracks,** and hospitals could prevent these diseases from occurring.

Florence's talent for mathematics was put to good use. She used statistics to prepare diagrams that showed the causes of death among the soldiers who had served in the Crimean War.

PARTHENOPE'S MARRIAGE

In 1858, Florence's sister, Parthenope, married Sir Harry Verney and became Lady Verney. Parthenope was 39 years old at the time. They lived in a mansion called Claydon House, in Buckinghamshire, England. Parthenope became a popular hostess, and rich and important people came to her parties. She wrote stories, and some were printed in magazines.

These British soldiers rest in army barracks in India.

Her statistical charts showed at a glance that most troops had died from preventable diseases. While 4,500 had been killed or died of wounds, a staggering 17,600 had died of disease.

Army officials saw that drastic changes were needed. As a direct result of Florence's work, by 1860 the Army Medical College had been established, and the hygiene of the army's barracks and hospitals had been improved.

Concerns for India

Florence's pioneering work was felt as far away as India, ruled by Britain at the time, where **regiments** of the British army were stationed. Improvements in hygiene were made there, too, and for the rest of her life, Florence remained interested in the state of India's sanitation. Though she never visited India, she wrote reports and issued guidelines that helped the nation to improve the health of its population.

In Nightingale's words:

"No one can feel for the army as I do. People must have seen that long dreadful winter to know what it was. I can never forget."

(From a letter to her sister, Parthenope, March 1856)

The Nightingale Nurses

Florence was always busy working on new ideas. One idea had been with her since before she went to Turkey: she wanted to set up a training school for nurses. There was little she could do about it while she was away from Britain, but in spite of this, a meeting was held in her absence.

THE NIGHTINGALE FUND.

THE signal services rendered by Miss NIGHTINGALE, to the sick and wounded of the British Forces in the East, have excited throughout the country a universal desire to testify by some marked and substantial acknowledgment, the gratitude and admiration of the British people.

But Miss NIGHTINGALE has nobly refused to accept any testimonial from which she could derive personal advantage of any description; while it is ascertained that the tribute most in harmony with her feelings and wishes, would be to afford further scope for her disinterested exertions by placing under her immediate superintendance the establishment of an Institution for the reception, protection, and training, of Hospital Nurses and Assistants, whereby the inestimable blessings of the system she has introduced, may be perpetuated and extended generally to the Poor, who may be suffering from sickness or accident.

To effect this object a public appeal has been made, to which the noble, the wealthy, and the benevolent, have liberally responded. But it is felt, that opportunity should not be denied to any class to manifest the sympathy all are known to entertain towards their devoted and highminded Countrywoman. The contributions, however small, of those who are dependent upon their labor, will have a peculiar fitness when given for an object by which the necessitous are to be exclusively benefited; while it is certain the widow's mite will have equal value in the estimation of Miss NIGHTINGALE, with the largest gifts of the great and the affluent.

Partaking in these views, the Proprietors of this Establishment have given permission for a Subscription Book to be opened in the Counting-House where any contributions however small, will be received and recorded; and the amount collected will be transmitted to the Committee and advertised as the contribution of the Workmen and others in this Establishment.

December 28th 1855.

This poster explains the purpose of the Nightingale Fund. Signs like this were displayed in banks and handed out at bookstores.

The Nightingale Fund

About nine months before Florence returned from the Crimea, more than 1,000 people had squeezed into a hall in London. They had come to hear plans to set up a fund, called the Nightingale Fund, to raise money for the training of nurses. Within three weeks, 20,000 letters had been sent out asking for money. By June 1856, the fund contained enough money to begin work on the first nurses' training school in England. The fund also increased people's awareness that nursing was a suitable occupation for respectable, educated women, and that nurses needed to be properly trained.

The Nightingale Training School

St. Thomas's Hospital, London, was chosen as the site for the new training school. Florence had been impressed by the **matron** there, Mrs. Sarah Wardroper, and felt she was the only person who could take charge of the nurses' training.

On June 24, 1860, nearly four years after Florence's return to Britain, the first group of fifteen trainee nurses, called **probationers,** began their studies at the Nightingale Training School. The nurses who attended the school became known as the Nightingale Nurses.

Mrs. Sarah Wardroper, the matron at St. Thomas's Hospital, was chosen by Florence to train the first Nightingale Nurses.

They trained for a year, had their own rooms, and were provided with brown uniforms and white caps and aprons. When their training was over, they were sent to work in hospitals in Britain and abroad. Some set up new schools to teach nursing.

In Nightingale's words:

"The Matron of that Hospital is the only one of any existing Hospital that I would recommend to form a school... for Nurses.... It will be beginning in a very humble way."

(From a letter to Sidney Herbert, indicating that St. Thomas's Hospital should be the place for the first school for nurses, May 24, 1859)

The Nightingale Training School owed much to Florence, yet she had little to do with it once it was established. She only visited it once, in 1886, but every year for thirty years, she wrote a letter of advice and encouragement to the nurses.

Florence the Writer

It has been estimated that Florence wrote 13,000 letters, and more than 200 articles, pamphlets, reports, and books—in addition to all the private notes she had written since childhood. At the end of 1859, she published a short book called *Notes on Nursing: What it is, and what it is not.* With a title like that, no one had any doubts what it was about, and it became very popular.

The pages of *Notes on Nursing* were filled with Florence's wisdom, based on her experience of nursing. Only she had the firsthand knowledge to write such a book. She did not mean it to be a nurse's instruction manual, though. In the book's preface, she wrote: "I do not pretend to teach her how, I ask her to teach herself, and for this purpose I venture to give her some hints." Florence, as usual, was being modest—the nurses who read the book cannot have failed to learn from it.

For my dear Beatrice from her loving Flo. New Year's Day 1860

NOTES ON NURSING:

WHAT IT IS, AND WHAT IT IS NOT.

BY

FLORENCE NIGHTINGALE.

LONDON:
HARRISON, 59, PALL MALL,
BOOKSELLER TO THE QUEEN.

Notes on Nursing *was Florence's most famous book. It has been translated into many foreign languages.*

In Nightingale's words:

"The fidget of silk and crinoline, the rattling of keys, the creaking of stays [corsets] and of shoes, will do a patient more harm than all the medicines in the world will do him good."

(From the chapter "Noise;" *Notes on Nursing,* 1859)

Observation and sensitivity

Notes on Nursing contained chapters with titles such as "Health of Houses," "Bed and Bedding," "Personal Cleanliness," and "What Food?" It outlined two of the most important principles of nursing—observation and sensitivity to a patient's needs. Observation, said Florence, was how the nurse gathered her facts. The nurse should observe things about a patient such as pulse, appetite, and breathing. A patient's comforts were also very important—a nurse had to make sure the patient was not too hot or too cold, that the ward was not too noisy, and that there was plenty of fresh air. Much of what Florence wrote seems like common sense today, yet people at the time needed to be told about it.

These letters were written by Florence. She wrote neatly, with a steel-nibbed pen dipped in ink.

DOROTHEA DIX—AN AMERICAN NURSE

The 1860s saw the beginning of nursing as a profession in the United States. It was based on the pioneering work of Florence Nightingale. During the American Civil War (1861–65), Dorothea Dix (1802–87) became **superintendent** of female nurses. She was in charge of all women nurses working in army hospitals of the Union. Dorothea, like Florence, was opposed by male doctors, but she was able to convince them of the importance of nurses. She recruited more than 3,000 nurses during the Civil War.

Florence's Nurses

Florence, age 66, was photographed with a group of Nightingale Nurses in 1886.

Every ten years, a **census** is held in many countries to find out how many people there are in the country, where they live, and what work they do. At the back of *Notes on Nursing,* Florence included information from the 1851 British census. It showed there were 25,466 women in Britain who said they worked as nurses. But what the census could not show was how good these nurses were at their work. Some may have been so-called "old-style" nurses, who had given nursing a poor reputation before Florence's **reforms.** "Old-style" nurses were untrained workers who knew little about nursing. They were criticized for being untidy and uncaring, sometimes doing more harm than good. Florence's fascination with **statistics** was, once again, put to good use. She used the census information to show that nursing was mostly for older women. In 1851, most nurses were between the ages of 50 and 60—and 147 were over 85!

This is the timetable for trainee nurses at the Nightingale Training School in 1862:

DAY DUTY										
6 A.M.	6:30 A.M.	7 A.M.	1 P.M.	2 P.M.	3:30 P.M.	5 P.M.	6 P.M.	8:30 P.M.	9 P.M.	10 P.M.
Rise	Breakfast	Wards	Dinner	Wards	Exercise	Tea	Wards	Dormitory	Supper	Bed

NIGHT DUTY										
9 P.M.	9:30 P.M.	10 P.M.	6 A.M.	6:30 A.M.	7 A.M.	10 A.M.	11 A.M.	1 P.M.	2 P.M.	
Rise	Tea	Wards	Dormitory	Breakfast	Wards	Dormitory	Exercise	Dinner	Bed	

The first Nightingale Nurses

The fifteen trainee nurses who entered the Nightingale Training School in June 1860 were younger women, between the ages of 22 and 40. They had been chosen because of their seemingly good characters. However, four were asked to leave before the end of their year's training—one because of illness, two because they had been disobedient, and one for drunkenness! Since Florence intended to make nursing a respectable, modern profession, drinking alcohol while on duty had to stop. That behavior belonged to the bad days of "old-style" nursing.

Florence drew up a personal record sheet for every trainee. The **matron,** Mrs. Wardroper, filled it in, noting such things as the trainee's punctuality, trustworthiness, cleanliness, and honesty. The trainee's nursing skills in bandaging; making beds; applying medicinal leeches, blood-sucking worms used to extract patients' blood; and observing the sick were also noted. Florence knew that if her reforms were to succeed, her nurses must be good at their work, and have good characters, too.

Florence gave gifts, such as books and nursing instruments, to the nurses who trained at the Nightingale Training School.

Florence and St. Thomas's Hospital

Florence began her long association with St. Thomas's Hospital in 1860, when it became home to the Nightingale Training School. At one time, she imagined she would spend the rest of her life at the hospital, living quietly into old age in a side room. But this was not to be.

Florence's London home

Since Florence's return to Britain from the Crimea in 1856, she had never had a home of her own. Instead, she had lived in hotels, in rented rooms, and in her parents' homes at Embley Park and Lea Hurst. All this changed in 1865, when her father bought her a house in the center of London, at 10 South Street. Florence settled in, with servants to help her and cats for company. A room in her home was also her office.

A new Nightingale Training School

Meanwhile, St. Thomas's Hospital had continued to expand, and by the late 1860s, it had outgrown its location. It was decided to build a new hospital. Florence was in her late 40s, and she regarded herself as old—yet despite her poor health, she took an interest in the design of the building. She was determined that the new hospital should be built to the highest, most **hygienic** standards of the day. In 1868, Queen Victoria laid the foundation stone for the new hospital, but Florence was too ill to attend.

> **In Nightingale's words:**
>
> *"It is always cheaper to build a good hospital than a bad one."*
>
> (From a letter to her brother-in-law, Sir Harry Verney)

St. Thomas's Hospital looked like this from the outside during the late 1800s.

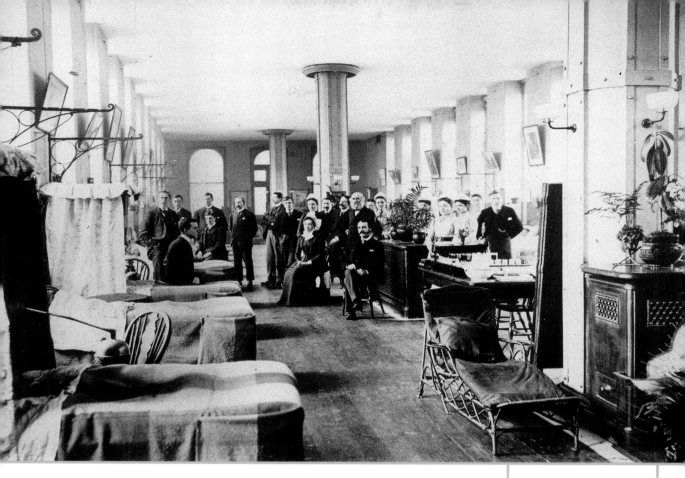

Three years later, when the building was completed in June 1871, the queen returned to declare the new St. Thomas's open. It included a larger Nightingale Training School, and Florence said this should be much more than a place of study. She wanted it to be a "home" for the nurses who lived and trained there. Florence arranged for the trainee nurses to attend Bible classes and listen to music, and encouraged them to read popular books of the day. She wanted to broaden their educations.

The wide spacing of the beds in this ward at St. Thomas's Hospital in 1890 was one of the changes brought about by Florence's *reforms.*

LINDA RICHARDS—FIRST TRAINED NURSE IN THE U.S.

The first training school for nurses in the U.S. was established in the early 1870s in Boston. The first nurse to qualify there was Linda Richards (1841–1930), recognized as the country's first trained nurse. Linda went on to work at the Bellevue Hospital in New York City, where she met Sister Helen, a nun who had trained in London as a Nightingale Nurse. In 1877, Linda studied at St. Thomas's Hospital in London. During her six months in Britain, she met Florence Nightingale and visited other hospitals. She used her experience to set up nurse training schools in the U.S. and Japan.

Florence's Last Years

By the 1870s, Florence's most important work had been done. Her busy life slowed down as the **reforms** she had begun in nursing and hospitals became standard practice, and as other people carried on her work.

Still helping

In 1874, Florence's father died. For the next six years, Florence put aside her work to care for her elderly and infirm mother, whom she nursed at Lea Hurst, the family home in Derbyshire. Her mother died there in 1880. Florence, then almost 60, returned to London, to her house in South Street.

In spite of her age and poor health, Florence still wanted to help people. Her doctor had told her to rest for a year, but for Florence this was impossible to do. She had given her life to serving the needy and she could not stop now. Ignoring her doctor's instructions, Florence resumed her work. She watched over the Nightingale Training School, she renewed her interest in India and the health of the people who lived there, and she became interested in the health of the British army in Africa. Florence even helped to care for her sister, Parthenope—who suffered from arthritis later in life—until she died in 1890. For as long as she could, Florence was determined to help others.

This photograph of Florence was taken when she was 71 years old.

Failing health

Florence began to lose her eyesight when she was in her 80s. By 1901, she was completely blind. Her memory began to fail, too. She was cared for at home. Visitors still came to see her, and the government sometimes asked for her advice on matters to do with public health.

In old age, Florence received many awards. In 1907, King Edward VII gave her the **Order of Merit**—a great honor for a British citizen. Florence, the first woman ever to receive it, earned the award "in recognition of invaluable services to the country and to humanity." The next year, she was granted the **Freedom of the City** of London. Women who had been named "Florence" in her honor sent letters, and old soldiers who had fought in the Crimean War said they had never forgotten her.

This message of congratulations to Florence came from the nurses of South Australia in 1904.

Florence died peacefully on August 13, 1910, at the age of 90. She was buried in the family grave in the village of East Wellow. On the day of the funeral, a service was held in St. Paul's Cathedral in London, attended by **veterans** of the Crimean War and 1,000 nurses. They had come to remember the "lady with a lamp." For them, and for countless thousands of others across the world, that flame would never die.

The Legacy of Florence Nightingale

Before Florence Nightingale pushed for change in the hospitals of the British army, nursing was a disorganized profession. Nurses' lack of training often did more harm than good. Florence made it her life's work to **reform** nursing and health care. She looked at the way hospitals were run and studied facts carefully to develop an improved system of nursing. She turned nursing into the respectable profession it is today.

A legacy of change

One of Florence Nightingale's greatest reforms was that she created new ways of working for nurses. Today's nurses do their jobs effectively and efficiently because Florence considered nurses' needs.

Florence also raised standards of care to a high level. Today's nurses are professional people whose duty it is to give patients the best possible care. Florence pioneered the use of **statistics** and graphs in health care.

These forms of communication are regularly used today to see changes in the condition of a patient at a glance. Florence showed how observation, or carefully watching patients for signs of their needs, was a key feature of nursing. Nurses today routinely monitor and manage their patients' needs, checking up on them regularly.

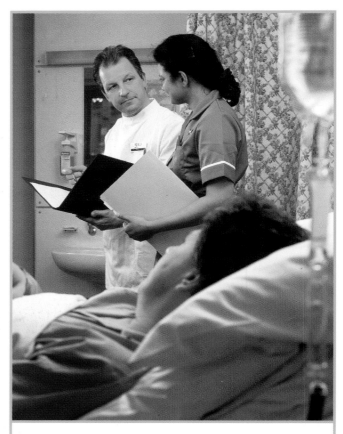

Men as well as women work as hospital nurses today.

In Nightingale's words:

"When I am no longer even a memory, just a name, I hope my voice may perpetuate the great work of my life. God bless my dear old comrades of Balaclava and bring them safe to shore."

(A sound recording of Florence's voice was made in London in 1890. These are her only recorded spoken words.)

She demonstrated that a healthy environment was good for a patient, and that comforting and caring for a patient is at the center of all good health care. This is as true today as it was in Florence's time.

Florence showed how health care reforms can come about as the result of people working together to solve a problem. Nothing is ever finished, and what Florence began is continually being improved by her successors in hospitals around the world today. For example, she believed in the need to train nurses. Today's nurses are trained in schools of nursing. After graduating, nurses regularly attend courses to bring them up to date with the latest nursing practices and methods.

Florence's attention to detail was incredible. She did not stop at improving nurses' skills, but also influenced the design of hospitals. Today's buildings are partly the result of Florence's ideas. They are built from **hygienic** materials, and wards are designed so that a nurse can see every patient easily.

Florence Nightingale influenced health care around the world in the nineteenth and twentieth centuries. Her achievements are even greater when we consider that she worked at a time when society was not used to women who were capable reformers. All this adds up to a huge legacy. Now, as the twenty-first century begins, the lessons learned from Florence's work are as relevant as they were then.

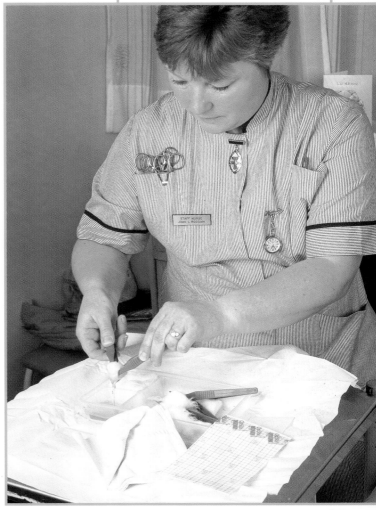

Today's nurses are highly skilled people.

Timeline

1820	Florence Nightingale born in Florence, Italy.
1821	Nightingale returns to Britain with her family.
	They settle in Derbyshire in a new house called Lea Hurst.
1825	The family move to a larger house, Embley Park in Hampshire.
1832	Nightingale's father begins to educate her at home.
1837	Nightingale believes she hears the voice of God.
	She travels to Europe with her family.
1839	Nightingale returns to Britain and **"comes out."**
1842	Meets Richard Monckton Milnes.
	Learns about the hospital at Kaiserswerth, Prussia.
1844	Asks a family friend about devoting her life to nursing.
	Declines a proposal of marriage from Henry Nicholson.
1845	Parents refuse to let her train to be a nurse at Salisbury Infirmary.
1846	Starts to become a self-taught expert on hospitals and **sanitation.**
1847	Becomes ill and is close to having a **nervous breakdown.**
	Goes to Italy with Charles and Selina Bracebridge.
	Meets Sidney and Elizabeth Herbert.
1849	Declines to marry Richard Monckton Milnes.
	Close to another nervous breakdown, she again travels abroad with the Bracebridges.
1850	Makes her first visit to the hospital at Kaiserswerth.
1851	Returns to Kaiserswerth and stays for three months, training to be a nurse.
1853	Given a yearly allowance by her father.
	Accepts her first job, as **superintendent** of the Institution for the Care of Sick Gentlewomen in Distressed Circumstances, London.
1854	Crimean War begins.
	Asked by Sidney Herbert, the government's **secretary-at-war,** to take charge of the army's hospitals in Turkey.
	Travels to the Barrack Hospital at Scutari, Turkey.
1855	Visits the Crimea and contracts "Crimean fever."
	Plans are made in London to set up the Nightingale Fund.
1856	Crimean War ends and Florence returns to Britain.
	Meets Queen Victoria and Prince Albert.
1857	Gathers a huge amount of information on the health of the army.
	Becomes aware of the need to improve the public health of India.
1858	Completes *Notes on Matters affecting the Health, Efficiency and Hospital Administration of the British Army.*

1859	Publishes a small book called *Notes on Nursing*.
1860	Nightingale Training School for nurses opens at St. Thomas's Hospital, London.
	Army Medical College opens, at Chatham, Kent.
1865	Moves to 10 South Street, London.
1874	Father dies.
1880	Mother dies.
1883	Nightingale is awarded the Royal Red Cross.
1890	Sister Parthenope dies.
1907	Becomes the first woman to receive the **Order of Merit.**
1908	Given the **Freedom of the City** of London.
1910	Death of Florence Nightingale.

More Books to Read

Colver, Anne. *Florence Nightingale: War Nurse.* Broomall, Pa.: Chelsea House Publishers, 1992.

Gorrell, Gena K. *Heart and Soul: The Story of Florence Nightingale.* Plattsburgh, N.Y.: Tundra Books Inc.: 2000.

Glossary

ambassador person who represents one country's government to that of another country

archaeology study of the past by examining the remains of ancient civilizations and cultures

aristocrat person belonging to the upper class, who is usually wealthy and owns land

barracks building or group of buildings used to house soldiers

bronchitis disease, not usually fatal, that affects a person's air passages and lungs, causing coughs, colds, and fevers

cavalry soldiers who ride and fight on horseback

census periodic count of the population of a place

cholera often fatal disease that causes diarrhea, vomiting, and cramping

"coming out" time at which a girl in her late teens or early twenties was presented by her parents at parties, signifying her passage from childhood to adulthood

convalescing recovering after an illness or accident

"Crimean fever" general name given to a number of diseases that affected people during the Crimean War

deaconess Christian woman who serves the needs of a community, offering help with things like health care and education

dispatch communication sent by a reporter to a newspaper

doctress woman who heals the sick, especially in societies that believe in the healing powers of plants and minerals

dysentery disease of the intestines causing stomach pain and severe diarrhea

epidemic widespread outbreak of a disease that affects many people in one place at the same time

Freedom of the City honor given to a person by a British city in recognition for services to the country

governess woman who teaches children in their own home

hygiene science of protecting people's health through cleanliness

lint linen or cotton material used for dressing wounds

matron woman in charge of nursing at a hospital

nervous breakdown weakness and exhaustion, often due to too much work or stress, that leaves a person unable to cope with the pressures of daily life

orderly attendant who works in a hospital

Order of Merit award to a British citizen from the king or queen in recognition of services to the country and to humanity

peninsula piece of land almost completely surrounded by water

philanthropist wealthy person who gives money to good causes for the benefit of others

philosophy use of reason and argument to seek truth and knowledge

post-traumatic stress disorder (PTSD) condition experienced by people after they have witnessed or been involved in a life-threatening event

prejudice poor opinion of something or someone, made ahead of time without knowing all the facts

privileged wealthy and fortunate

probationer name given to a trainee nurse at the Nightingale Training School

reform to change the way things are done

reformer person who seeks to change things for the better

regiment large unit of an army, made up of smaller units called battalions

royal commission group of people chosen by a government to investigate something of national importance

Sanitary Commission group set up by the government to investigate public health

sanitation process of protecting public health by improving things such as drainage and trash disposal

scholar student; also a well-educated, clever person

secretary-at-war in Victorian Britain, a government minister with responsibility for the armed forces

statistics science dealing with collecting and studying numerical data

superintendent person who has overall control of a place or organization and the people who work within it

telegraph system for transmitting messages using electricity

typhoid infectious fever, caused by bacteria, that produces a rash and irritation of the intestines

veteran person who has served in the military

Index

Feb 7

28 DAY LOAN